Collins

SNAP REVISION

BONDING, STRUCTURE AND PROPERTIES OF MATTER & QUANTITATIVE CHEMISTRY

AQA GCSE Chemistry

C000109239

AQA
GCSE
CHEMISTRY

REVISE TRICKY TOPICS IN A SNAP

PROPERTIES OF MATTER & QUANTITATIVE CHEMISTRY

Contents

Published by Collins
An imprint of HarperCollinsPublishers
1 London Bridge Street,
London, SE1 9GF

© HarperCollinsPublishers Limited 2016

9780008218119

First published 2016

10 9 8 7 6 5 4 3 2 1

All rights reserved. No part of this publication may be
reproduced, stored in a retrieval system, or transmitted,
in any form or by any means, electronic, mechanical,
photocopying, recording or otherwise, without the prior
permission of Collins.

British Library Cataloguing in Publication Data.
A CIP record of this book is available from the British Library.
Printed in United Kingdom by Martins the Printers

ACKNOWLEDGEMENTS
The author and publisher are grateful to the copyright
holders for permission to use quoted materials and images.
pEvery effort has been made to trace copyright holders and
obtain their permission for the use of copyright material.
The author and publisher will gladly receive information
enabling them to rectify any error or omission in subsequent
editions. All facts are correct at time of going to press.

HT Higher Tier content

How To Use This Book

To get the most out of this revision guide, just work your way through the book in the order it is presented.

This is how it works:

Revise

Clear and concise revision notes help you get to grips with the topic

Revise

Key Points and Key Words explain the important information you need to know

Revise

A Quick Test at the end of every topic is a great way to check your understanding

Practise

Practice questions for each topic reinforce the revision content you have covered

Review

The Review section is a chance to revisit the topic to improve your recall in the exam

States of Matter

You must be able to:

- Recall the meaning of the state symbols in equations
- Describe how the particles move in solids, liquids and gases
- Use the particle model to explain how the particles are arranged in the three states of matter
- **HT** Describe the limitations of the particle model.

Three States of Matter

- Everything is made of matter.
- There are three states of matter: solid, liquid and gas.
- These three states of matter are described by a simple model called the 'particle model'.
- In this model, the particles are represented by small solid spheres.
- The model can be used to explain how the particles are arranged and how they move in solids, liquids and gases.
- In solids, the particles:
  - have a regular arrangement
  - are very close together
  - vibrate about fixed positions.
- In liquids, the particles:
  - have a random arrangement
  - are close together
  - flow around each other.
- In gases, the particles:
  - have a random arrangement
  - are much further apart
  - move very quickly in all directions.

Solid

Liquid

Gas

 Key Point

This particle model does have some limitations. It does not take into account:

- the forces between the particles
- the volume (although small) of the particles
- the space between particles.

Changing States

- When a substance changes state, e.g. from solid to liquid:
  - the particles themselves stay the same
  - the way the particles are arranged changes
  - the way the particles move changes.
- A pure substance will:
  - melt and freeze at one specific temperature – the melting point
  - boil and condense at one specific temperature – the boiling point.
- The amount of energy required for a substance to change state depends on the amount of energy required to overcome the forces of attraction between the particles.
- The stronger the forces of attraction:
  - the greater the amount of energy needed to overcome them
  - the higher the melting point and boiling point will be.
- Substances that have high melting points due to strong bonds include ionic compounds, metals and giant covalent structures.

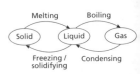

- In substances that contain simple molecules:
  - the bonds within the molecules are strong covalent bonds
  - the forces of attraction between the molecules are much weaker
  - only a little energy is needed to overcome the forces between the molecules, so the melting and boiling points are relatively low.

Identifying the State of a Substance

- The melting point and boiling point of a substance can be used to identify its state at a given temperature.

> **Key Point**
>
> The stronger the forces between particles, the higher the melting point of the substance.

The table below shows the melting points and boiling points of some Group 7 elements.

What is the state of each element at 25°C (room temperature)?

Element	Melting Point (°C)	Boiling Point (°C)
fluorine	−220	−188
chlorine	−102	−34
bromine	−7	59
iodine	114	184

> 25°C is above the boiling points of fluorine and chlorine, so they will be gases.
>
> 25°C is above the melting point but below the boiling point of bromine, so it will be a liquid.
>
> 25°C is below the melting point of iodine, so it will be a solid.

Fluorine and chlorine are gases, bromine is a liquid and iodine is a solid.

State Symbols

- Chemical equations are used to sum up what happens in reactions.
- State symbols show the state of each substance involved.

State Symbol	State of Substance
(s)	solid
(l)	liquid
(g)	gas
(aq)	aqueous (dissolved in water)

- For example, when solid magnesium ribbon is added to an aqueous solution of hydrochloric acid:
  - a chemical reaction takes place
  - a solution of magnesium chloride is produced
  - hydrogen gas is produced.
- This can be summed up in a symbol equation:

$$Mg(s) + 2HCl(aq) \longrightarrow MgCl_2(aq) + H_2(g)$$

> **Quick Test**
>
> 1. What does the state symbol (l) indicate?
> 2. What does the state symbol (aq) indicate?
> 3. How do the particles in a gas move?
> 4. Why do ionic compounds have high melting points?
> 5. State three limitations of the particle model.

> **Key Words**
>
> matter
> particle
> melting point
> boiling point
> aqueous

Ionic Compounds

You must be able to:

- Describe what an ionic bond is
- Explain how ionic bonding involves the transfer of electrons from metal atoms to non-metal atoms to form ions
- Relate the properties of ionic compounds to their structures.

Chemical Bonds

- There are three types of strong chemical bonds:
  - ionic bonds
  - covalent bonds
  - metallic bonds.
- Atoms that have gained or lost electrons are called ions.
- Ionic bonds occur between positive and negative ions.

Ionic Bonding

- Ions are formed when atoms gain or lose electrons, giving them an overall charge.
- Ions have a complete outer shell of electrons (the same electronic structure as a noble gas).
- Ionic bonding involves a transfer of electrons from metal atoms to non-metal atoms.
- The metal atoms lose electrons to become positively charged ions.
- The non-metal atoms gain electrons to become negatively charged ions.
- The ionic bond is a strong electrostatic force of attraction between the positive metal ion and the negative non-metal ion.

> **Key Point**
>
> The arrangement of electrons in an atom can be described in terms of shells or energy levels. Electron configuration diagrams are a good example of using diagrams to represent information.

● Positively charged ion ● Negatively charged ion

Sodium forms an ionic compound with chlorine.

Describe what happens when two atoms of sodium react with one molecule of chlorine.

Give your answer in terms of electron transfer.

- Sodium belongs to Group 1 of the periodic table. It has one electron in its outer shell.
- Chlorine belongs to Group 7 of the periodic table. It has seven electrons in its outer shell.
- One chlorine molecule contains two chlorine atoms.
- Each sodium atom transfers one electron to one of the chlorine atoms.
- All four atoms now have eight electrons in their outer shell.
- The atoms become ions, Na^+ and Cl^-.
- The compound formed is sodium chloride, $NaCl$.

$$2Na + Cl_2 \rightarrow 2NaCl$$

Electron

Na atom 2,8,1   Cl atom 2,8,7

Na$^+$ ion [2,8]$^+$ Cl$^-$ ion [2,8,8]$^-$

When magnesium is burned, it forms an ionic compound with oxygen.

Describe what happens when two atoms of magnesium react with one molecule of oxygen. Give your answer in terms of electron transfer.

- Magnesium is in Group 2 of the periodic table. It has two electrons in its outer shell.
- Oxygen is in Group 6 of the periodic table. It has six electrons in its outer shell.
- One oxygen molecule contains two oxygen atoms.
- Each magnesium atom loses two electrons to an oxygen atom.
- All four atoms now have eight electrons in their outer shell.
- The atoms become ions, Mg^{2+} and O^{2-}.
- The compound formed is magnesium oxide, MgO.

$$2Mg + O_2 \rightarrow 2MgO$$

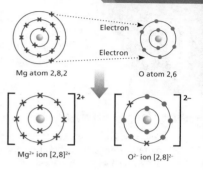

Mg atom 2,8,2   O atom 2,6

Mg^{2+} ion $[2,8]^{2+}$ O^{2-} ion $[2,8]^{2-}$

Properties of Ionic Compounds

- Ionic compounds are giant structures of ions.
- They are held together by strong forces of attraction (electrostatic forces) that act in all directions between oppositely charged ions, i.e. ionic compounds are held together by strong ionic bonds.
- Ionic compounds:
  - have high melting and boiling points
  - do *not* conduct electricity when solid, because the ions cannot move
  - do conduct electricity when **molten** or in solution, because the charged ions are free to move about and carry their charge.

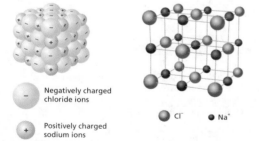

Negatively charged chloride ions

Positively charged sodium ions

 Cl^- ● Na^+

Key Point

An ionic bond is the attraction between oppositely charged ions.

Key Point

Ionic compounds have high melting and boiling points because ionic bonds are very strong and it requires lots of energy to overcome them.

Quick Test

1. What is an ion?
2. Why do metals form positively charged ions?
3. The ionic compound potassium chloride contains potassium ions (K^+) and chloride ions (Cl^-). What is the formula of potassium chloride?
4. Why do ionic compounds conduct electricity when molten?

Key Words

ionic bond
ion
electrostatic
molten

Metals

You must be able to:

- Describe when and why metallic bonding occurs
- Explain why metals conduct electricity
- Describe and explain the properties of pure metals and alloys.

Metallic Bonding

- Metallic bonding occurs in:
  - metallic elements, such as iron and copper
  - alloys, such as stainless steel.
- Metals have a giant structure in which electrons in the outer shell are delocalised (not bound to one atom).
- This produces a regular arrangement (lattice) of positive ions held together by electrostatic attraction to the delocalised electrons.
- A metallic bond is the attraction between the positive ions and the delocalised negatively charged electrons.

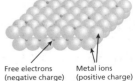

Free electrons   Metal ions
(negative charge)   (positive charge)

Properties of Metals

- The properties of metals make them very useful.
- Metallic bonds are very strong and most metals have high melting and boiling points. This means that they are useful structural materials.
- The delocalised electrons can move around freely and transfer energy. This makes metals good thermal and electrical conductors.
- The particles in pure metals have a regular arrangement.
- The layers are able to slide over each other quite easily, which means that metals can be bent and shaped.
- Traditionally, copper is used to make water pipes because:
  - it is an unreactive metal, so it does not react with water
  - it can be easily shaped.

> ### Key Point
>
> A metallic bond is the attraction between positive ions and delocalised electrons.

Metal	Uses	Property
Aluminium	High-voltage power cables, furniture, drinks cans, foil food wrap	Corrosion resistant, ductile, malleable, good conductivity, low density
Copper	Electrical wiring, water pipes, saucepans	Ductile, malleable, good conductivity
Gold	Jewellery, electrical junctions	Ductile, shiny, good conductivity

Alloys

- Most metal objects are made from alloys – mixtures that contain a metal and at least one other element.
- Pure metals are too soft for many uses.
- In alloys, the added element disturbs the regular arrangement of the metal atoms so the layers do not slide over each other so easily.
- This means alloys are usually stronger and harder than pure metals.

Steel

- Steel is a very useful alloy made from iron.
- Iron oxide can be reduced in a blast furnace to produce iron.
- Molten iron obtained from a blast furnace contains roughly 96% iron and 4% impurities, including carbon, phosphorus and silica.
- Because it is impure, the iron is very brittle and has limited uses.
- To produce pure iron, all the impurities have to be removed.
- The atoms in pure iron are arranged in layers that can slide over each other easily, making it soft and malleable.
- Pure iron can be easily shaped, but it is too soft for many practical uses.
- The properties of iron can be changed by mixing it with small quantities of carbon or other metals to make steel.
- The majority of iron is converted into steel.
- Alloys are developed to have the required properties for a specific purpose.
- In steel, the amount of carbon and / or other elements determines its properties:
  - Steel with a high carbon content is hard and strong.
  - Steel with a low carbon content is soft and easily shaped.
  - Stainless steel contains chromium and nickel and is hard and resistant to corrosion.

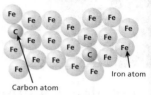

Steel

Carbon atom

Iron atom

HT Other Useful Alloys

- Pure copper, gold and aluminium are too soft for many uses.
- They are mixed with small amounts of similar metals to make them harder for items in everyday use, e.g. coins.
- Gold is mixed with silver, copper and zinc to form an alloy.
- The carat system shows the amount of gold in the alloy:
  - 24 carat gold is 100% gold
  - 18 carat gold is $\frac{18}{24} \times 100\% = 75\%$ gold.
- Aluminium alloys combine low density with high strength and are used to make aeroplanes.
- Bronze is an alloy of copper and tin.
- It has a bright gold colour and is used to make statues and decorative objects.
- Brass is an alloy of copper and zinc that is hard-wearing and very resistant to corrosion.
- It is used to make water taps and door fittings.

Key Words

delocalised
electrostatic
metallic bond
pure
ductile
malleable
alloy
brittle
corrosion

Quick Test

1. Describe what a metallic bond is.
2. Why is copper a good material for water pipes?
3. What is an alloy?
4. Why are alloys more useful than pure metals?
5. Give two useful properties that stainless steel has but pure iron does not have.

Covalent Compounds

You must be able to:

- Describe a covalent bond
- Describe the structure of simple molecules
- Explain the properties of simple molecules
- Describe the giant covalent structures: diamond, graphite and silicon dioxide
- Explain the properties of giant covalent structures.

Covalent Bonding

- A covalent bond is a shared pair of electrons between atoms.
- Covalent bonds occur in:
  - non-metallic elements, e.g. oxygen, O_2
  - compounds of non-metals, e.g. sulfur dioxide, SO_2.
- For example, a chlorine atom has seven electrons in its outer shell. In order to bond with another chlorine atom:
  - an electron from each atom is shared
  - this gives each chlorine atom eight electrons in the outer shell
  - each atom now has a complete outer shell.
- Covalent bonds in molecules can be shown using dot and cross diagrams.
- Covalent bonds are very strong.
- Some covalently bonded substances have simple structures:

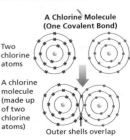

**A Chlorine Molecule
(One Covalent Bond)**

Two chlorine atoms

A chlorine molecule (made up of two chlorine atoms)

Outer shells overlap

**A Molecule of Ammonia
(Three Covalent Bonds)**

Molecule	Water H_2O	Hydrogen H_2	Hydrogen chloride, HCl	Methane CH_4	Oxygen O_2	Nitrogen N_2
Method 1	H O H	H H	H Cl	H C H (with H above and below)	O O	N N
Method 2	H–O–H	H–H	H–Cl	H–C–H (with H above and below)	O=O (a double bond)	N≡N (a triple bond)

- Others have giant covalent structures, e.g. diamond and silicon dioxide.

Simple Molecules

- Simple molecules contain a relatively small number of non-metal atoms joined together by covalent bonds.
- The molecules have no overall electrical charge, so they cannot conduct electricity.
- Substances that consist of simple molecules are usually liquids and gases that have relatively low melting and boiling points.
- This is because they have weak intermolecular forces (forces of attraction between the molecules).
- These intermolecular forces are very weak compared to the strength of the covalent bonds in the molecules themselves.

Key Point

Simple molecular substances, such as water, have low melting and boiling points. This is because there are only weak forces of attraction between the molecules, which are easily overcome.

- The larger the molecules are, the stronger the intermolecular forces between the molecules become.
- This means that larger molecules have higher melting and boiling points.
- Going down Group 7 of the periodic table, the molecules get larger and their melting and boiling points increase.
- This is demonstrated by their states at room temperature:
  - Fluorine and chlorine are gases.
  - Bromine is a liquid.
  - Iodine is a solid.

Strong covalent bond within the molecule

Weak forces of attraction between molecules

Giant Covalent Structures

- All the atoms in giant covalent structures are linked by strong covalent bonds.
- These bonds must be broken for the substance to melt or boil.
- This means that giant covalent structures are solids with very high melting and boiling points.
- Diamond is a form of carbon:
  - It has a giant, rigid covalent structure (lattice).
  - Each carbon atom forms four strong covalent bonds with other carbon atoms.
  - All the strong covalent bonds mean that it is a very hard substance with a very high melting point.
  - There are no charged particles, so it does not conduct electricity.
- Graphite is another form of carbon:
  - It also has a giant covalent structure and a very high melting point.
  - Each carbon atom forms three covalent bonds with other carbon atoms.
  - This results in a layered, hexagonal structure.
  - The layers are held together by weak intermolecular forces.
  - This means that the layers can slide past each other, making graphite soft and slippery.
  - One electron from each carbon atom in graphite is delocalised.
  - These delocalised electrons allow graphite to conduct heat and electricity.
- Silicon dioxide (or silica, SiO_2) has a lattice structure similar to diamond:
  - Each oxygen atom is joined to two silicon atoms.
  - Each silicon atom is joined to four oxygen atoms.

Diamond

Covalent bond between carbon atoms

◉ Carbon atom

Graphite

Covalent bond between carbon atoms

◉ Carbon atom

Weak bond between layers

---

1. What is a covalent bond?
2. Why does hydrogen chloride (HCl) have a low boiling point?
3. How does the size of a simple molecule affect the strength of the intermolecular forces between molecules?
4. Describe the structure of diamond.
5. Explain how graphite can conduct electricity.

Key Words

covalent bond
intermolecular
diamond
graphite
delocalised
silicon dioxide (silica)

Special Materials

You must be able to:

- Recall the structure and uses of graphene and fullerenes
- Recall the size of nanoparticles, fine particles and coarse particles
- Understand the bonding within and between polymer molecules
- Understand why nanoparticles have special properties.

Graphene

- Graphene is a form of carbon. It is a single layer of graphite (see page 11).
- The atoms are arranged in a hexagonal structure, just one atom thick.
- Graphene is very strong, a good thermal and electrical conductor and nearly transparent.
- These properties make graphene useful in electronics and composite materials.

Fullerenes

- Carbon can also form molecules known as fullerenes, which contain different numbers of carbon atoms.
- The structure of fullerenes is based on hexagonal rings of carbon atoms. Sometimes these rings contain five or seven carbon atoms.
- Fullerene molecules have hollow shapes, including tubes, balls and cages.
- The first fullerene to be discovered was buckminsterfullerene, C_{60}:
  - It consists of 60 carbon atoms.
  - The atoms are joined together in a series of hexagons and pentagons.
  - It is the most symmetrical and, therefore, most stable fullerene.
- Carbon nanotubes are cylindrical fullerenes with very high length to diameter ratios.
- The properties of carbon nanotubes make them very useful for use in nanotechnology, electronics and materials.
- Fullerenes can be used to deliver drugs in the body; in lubricants; as catalysts; for reinforcing materials, e.g. the frames of tennis rackets, so that they are strong but still lightweight.

Structure of Buckminsterfullerene

Carbon atom — Strong covalent bond

Structure of a Nanotube

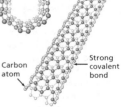

Carbon atom — Strong covalent bond

Polymers

- Polymers consist of very large molecules.
- Plastics are synthetic (man-made) polymers.
- The atoms within the polymer molecules are held together by strong covalent bonds.
- The intermolecular forces between the large polymer molecules are also quite strong.
- This means that polymers are solid at room temperature.
- Poly(ethene), commonly known as polythene, is produced when lots of ethene molecules are joined together in an addition polymerisation reaction. It is cheap and strong and is used to make plastic bottles and bags.

$$n \quad \begin{matrix} H \\ \diagdown \\ C \\ \diagup \\ H \end{matrix} = \begin{matrix} H \\ \diagup \\ C \\ \diagdown \\ H \end{matrix} \longrightarrow \left(\begin{matrix} H & H \\ | & | \\ -C - C - \\ | & | \\ H & H \end{matrix} \right)_n$$

Sizes of Particles and their Properties

- Coarse particles (often called 'dust' by scientists) have a diameter between 1×10^{-5}m and 2.5×10^{-6}m.
- Fine particles have a diameter between 100nm and 2500nm or 1×10^{-7}m and 2.5×10^{-6}m.
- Nanoparticles have a diameter between 1nm and 100nm or 1×10^{-9}m and 1×10^{-7}m.
- Nanoscience is the study of these very small structures.
- Small particles have a high surface area to volume ratio.
- Changing the size of particles has a dramatic effect on this ratio.
- For example, if the length of side of a cube decreases by a factor of 10:
  - the surface area decreases by $10 \times 10 = 100$
  - the volume decreases by $10 \times 10 \times 10 = 1000$
  - the surface area to volume ratio increases tenfold.
- This is important for catalysts, as having a large surface area improves their effectiveness.

Key Point

One nanometre is 0.000 000 001m (one billionth of a metre) and is written as 1nm or 1×10^{-9}m.

Nanoparticles

- Nanoparticles contain only a few hundred atoms.
- They can combine to form structures called nanostructures.
- Nanostructures can be manipulated, so materials can be developed that have new and specific properties.
- The properties of nanoparticles are different to the properties of the same materials in bulk, e.g. nanoparticles are more sensitive to light, heat and magnetism.
- In nanoparticles, the atoms can be placed into exactly the right position so smaller quantities are needed to achieve the required properties / effects.
- Nanoparticles are used in sun creams.
- They provide better skin coverage and, therefore, more effective protection from the sun's harmful ultraviolet rays.
- However, concerns remain that these nanoparticles are so small they could get into and damage human cells or cause problems in the environment.
- Research into nanoparticles is leading to the development of:
  - new drug delivery systems
  - synthetic skin for burn victims
  - computers and technology
  - catalysts for fuel cells
  - stronger and lighter construction materials
  - new cosmetics and deodorants
  - fabrics that prevent the growth of bacteria.

Key Point

The use of nanoparticles is a good example of a science-based technology, for which the hazards have to be considered alongside the benefits. However, because the technology is so new, data is uncertain and incomplete.

Quick Test

1. What is special about the structure of graphene?
2. Which is the most stable fullerene?
3. How big are nanoparticles?
4. What potential problems could nanoparticles cause?

Key Words

graphene
transparent
fullerene
nanoparticles

Practice Questions

States of Matter

1   State symbols are used to add extra information to equations.

    a) What does the state symbol (g) mean? [1]

    b) What does the state symbol (aq) mean? [1]

2   HT Give **three** limitations of the particle model. [3]

3   Calcium reacts with hydrochloric acid to produce calcium chloride and hydrogen.
The equation for the reaction is shown below:

$Ca(s) + 2HCl(aq) \rightarrow CaCl_2(aq) + H_2(g)$

What is the state of the:

    a) Calcium? [1]

    b) Hydrochloric acid? [1]

    c) Hydrogen? [1]

Total Marks .... / 8

Ionic Compounds

1   Sodium fluoride is an ionic compound.

    a) Suggest why sodium fluoride has a high melting point. [2]

    b) Does sodium fluoride conduct electricity when solid?
You must explain your answer. [1]

    c) Does sodium fluoride conduct electricity when molten?
You must explain your answer. [1]

    d) Does sodium fluoride conduct electricity when dissolved in water to form an
aqueous solution?
You must explain your answer. [1]

2 **Table 1** shows the charge on some metal ions and non-metal ions.

Table 1

Metal Ions	Non-Metal Ions
Sodium, Na^+	Chloride, Cl^-
Magnesium, Mg^{2+}	Oxide, O^{2-}
Potassium, K^+	Fluoride, F^-
Calcium, Ca^{2+}	Sulfide, S^{2-}

a) What is an ion? [1]

b) In terms of electron transfer, explain why chloride ions have a 1– charge. [2]

c) In terms of electron transfer, explain why magnesium ions have a 2+ charge. [2]

d) Use the information in the table to determine the formula of:

i) Potassium chloride [1]

ii) Magnesium sulfide [1]

iii) Calcium oxide. [1]

e) Magnesium oxide has a very high melting point and can be used to line furnaces.

Explain why the compound magnesium oxide has a high melting point. [2]

Total Marks _____ / 15

Metals

1 a) What is the chemical symbol for gold? [1]

b) Name the type of bonding that occurs in gold. [1]

c) Pure gold is too soft for many uses.

Why is pure gold soft? [2]

d) Gold is often made into an alloy.

What is an 'alloy'? [1]

e) Gold is used to make components for computers because it is a very good electrical conductor.

Why is gold a good electrical conductor? [2]

> Total Marks _____ / 7

Covalent Compounds

1 **Figure 1** shows the structure of diamond.

Figure 1

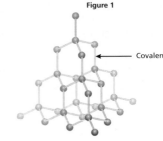

Covalent bond

a) Diamond is a form of which element? [1]

b) Why is diamond so hard? [1]

c) Why is diamond a poor electrical conductor? [1]

2 Methane molecules have the formula CH_4.

a) Explain why methane is a poor electrical conductor. [1]

b) Explain why methane has a low boiling point. [2]

3 **Figure 2** shows the outer electrons in a magnesium atom and in a sulfur atom.

Figure 2

a) **i)** In which group of the periodic table is magnesium? [1]

ii) In which group of the periodic table is sulfur? [1]

iii) Draw a diagram to show the outer electrons in a magnesium ion and in a sulfide ion. [2]

b) The compound magnesium sulfide is a solid at room temperature.

What type of structure does magnesium sulfide have?
Tick **one** box.

Giant metallic ☐   Giant covalent ☐

Simple molecular ☐   Giant ionic ☐   [1]

c) Explain why magnesium sulfide does not conduct electricity when solid.   [2]

4 Ammonia, NH_3, and water, H_2O, are both simple molecules.
Both of these compounds contain covalent bonds.

a) Define the term 'covalent bond'.   [1]

b) **Figure 3** shows the outer electrons in a nitrogen atom and in a hydrogen atom.

Figure 3

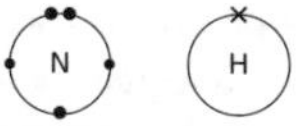

Complete **Figure 4** below to show the electron arrangement in an ammonia molecule.   [1]

Figure 4

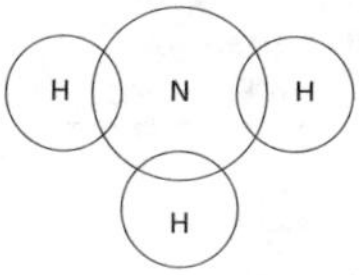

c) Explain why ammonia and water do **not** conduct electricity.   [1]

Total Marks _____ / 16

Special Materials

1 **a)** What size are nanoparticles?
Tick **one** box.

1 to 100nm ☐   1 to 10nm ☐

Less than 1nm ☐   100 to 1000nm ☐   [1]

b) Suggest a possible problem that nanoparticles could cause.   [1]

Total Marks _____ / 2

Conservation of Mass

You must be able to:

- Understand the law of conservation of mass
- Work out the relative formula mass of substances
- Understand why reactions that involve gases may appear to show a change in mass
- **HT** Write balanced half equations and ionic equations.

The Conservation of Mass

- In a chemical reaction, the total mass of the products is equal to the total mass of the reactants.
- This idea is called the conservation of mass.
- Mass is conserved (kept the same) because no atoms are lost or made.
- Chemical symbol equations must always be balanced to show this, i.e. there must be the same number of atoms of each element on both sides of the equation.
- For example, when solid iron reacts with copper(II) sulfate solution, a reaction takes place, producing solid copper and iron(II) sulfate solution:

$$Fe(s) + CuSO_4(aq) \longrightarrow Cu(s) + FeSO_4(aq)$$

HT A half equation can be used to show what happens to one reactant in a chemical reaction, with electrons written as e^-.

HT The balanced symbol equation for the reaction between iron and copper(II) sulfate can be split into two half equations:
- The iron atoms lose two electrons to form Fe^{2+} ions.

$$Fe(s) \longrightarrow Fe^{2+}(aq) + 2e^-$$

- The Cu^{2+} ions gain two electrons to form copper atoms.

$$Cu^{2+}(aq) + 2e^- \longrightarrow Cu(s)$$

HT Ionic equations can be used to simplify complicated equations.

HT They just show the species that are involved in the reaction.

HT The spectator ions (ions not involved in the reaction) are not included.

HT For example, when silver nitrate solution is added to sodium chloride solution, a white precipitate of silver chloride is produced:

$$AgNO_3(aq) + NaCl(aq) \longrightarrow AgCl(s) + NaNO_3(aq)$$

HT In this reaction, the nitrate ions and the sodium ions are spectator ions, so the ionic equation is:

$$Ag^+(aq) + Cl^-(aq) \longrightarrow AgCl(s)$$

HT In chemistry, the term 'species' refers to the different atoms, molecules or ions that are involved in a reaction.

> **Key Point**
>
> The total mass of the products of a chemical reaction is always equal to the total mass of the reactants. This is because no atoms are lost or made. The products are made from exactly the same atoms as the reactants.

Relative Formula Mass

- The relative formula mass (M_r) of a compound is the sum of the relative atomic masses (A_r) of all the atoms in the numbers shown in the formula. It does not have a unit.
- The relative atomic masses of the atoms are shown in the periodic table.

> What is the relative formula mass of carbon dioxide, CO_2?
> Relative formula mass $= (12 \times 1) + (16 \times 2)$
> $= 44$ ◄───

CO_2 contains 1 carbon atom with a relative atomic mass of 12 and 2 oxygen atoms with a relative atomic mass of 16.

> Calculate the relative formula mass of calcium nitrate, $Ca(NO_3)_2$.
> Relative formula mass $= 40 + (14 \times 2) + (16 \times 6)$
> $= 164$ ◄───

Remember that everything inside a set of brackets is multiplied by the number outside the brackets, so $Ca(NO_3)_2$ contains 1 calcium, 2 nitrogen and 6 oxygen atoms.

- Due to conservation of mass, the sum of the relative formula masses of all the reactants is always equal to the sum of the relative formula masses of all the products.

Apparent Changes in Mass

- Some reactions appear to involve a change in mass.
- This happens when reactions are carried out in a non-closed system and include a gas that can enter or leave.
- For example, when magnesium is burned in air to produce magnesium oxide, the mass of the solid increases.
- This is because when the magnesium is burned, it combines with oxygen from the air and the oxygen has mass:

$$2Mg(s) + O_2(g) \longrightarrow 2MgO(s)$$

- If the mass of oxygen is included, the total mass of all the reactants is equal to the total mass of all the products.
- When calcium carbonate is heated, it decomposes to form calcium oxide and carbon dioxide:

$$CaCO_3(s) \longrightarrow CaO(s) + CO_2(g)$$

- The mass of the solid decreases because one of the products is a gas, which escapes into the air.
- If the mass of carbon dioxide is included, the total mass of all the reactants is equal to the total mass of all the products.

Quick Test

1. State the law of conservation of mass.
2. Why must a symbol equation balance?
3. Calculate the relative formula mass of water, H_2O.
4. Calculate the relative formula mass of calcium carbonate, $CaCO_3$.
5. When iron is burned, iron oxide is produced and the mass of the solid increases. Why does the mass of the solid increase during this reaction?

Key Point

The relative atomic mass is an average value that takes account of the abundance of the isotopes of an element. 25% of chlorine atoms have a mass of 37. 75% of chlorine atoms have a mass of 35. The relative atomic mass of chlorine $=$
$(\frac{25}{100} \times 37) + (\frac{75}{100} \times 35)$
$= 35.5$

Key Point

Some reactions appear to involve a change in mass. This happens when reactions are carried out in a non-closed system, so gases can enter or leave.

Key Words

conservation of mass
HT half equation
HT ionic equation
HT species
relative formula mass (M_r)
relative atomic mass (A_r)

Amount of Substance

You must be able to:

- HT Recall the number of particles in one mole of any substance
- HT Calculate the amount of a substance in moles
- HT Calculate the mass of reactants or products from balanced equations
- HT Calculate the balancing numbers in equations from the masses of the reactants and the products by using moles
- HT Calculate the volume of a given amount of a gas.

Amount of Substance

- A mole (mol) is a measure of the number of particles (atoms, ions or molecules) contained in a substance.
- One mole of any substance (element or compound) contains the same number of particles – six hundred thousand billion billion or 6.02×10^{23}.
- This value is known as the Avogadro constant.
- The mass of one mole of a substance is its relative atomic mass or relative formula mass in grams.

> One mole of sodium atoms contains 6.02×10^{23} atoms.
> The relative atomic mass of sodium is 23.0.
> One mole of sodium atoms has a mass of 23.0g.

 Key Point

One mole of any substance (element or compound) will always contain the same number of particles – six hundred thousand billion billion or 6.02×10^{23}. This value is known as the Avogadro constant.

Calculating the Amount of Substance

- You can calculate the amount of substance (number of moles) in a given mass of a substance using the formula:

LEARN HT

$$\text{amount (mol)} = \frac{\text{mass of substance (g)}}{\text{atomic (or formula) mass (g/mol)}}$$

Calculate the number of moles of carbon dioxide in 33g of the compound.

$$\text{amount} = \frac{\text{mass of substance}}{\text{formula mass}}$$
$$= \frac{33}{44}$$
$$= 0.75\text{mol}$$

Formula mass = $12 + (16 \times 2)$
= 44

Balanced Equations

- Balanced equations:
  - show the number of moles of each product and reactant
  - can be used to calculate the mass of the reactants and products.
- The numbers needed to balance an equation can be calculated from the masses of the reactants and the products using moles.

Aluminium oxide can be reduced to produce aluminium:

$$Al_2O_3 \rightarrow 2Al + 1\tfrac{1}{2}O_2$$

Calculate the mass of aluminium oxide needed to produce 540g of aluminium.

$$\text{amount of aluminium} = \frac{540}{27} = 20\text{mol}$$

$$\text{amount of aluminium oxide required} = \frac{20}{2} = 10\text{mol}$$

$$\text{formula mass of aluminium oxide} = (27 \times 2) + (16 \times 3)$$
$$= 102$$

$$\text{mass of aluminium oxide needed} = 10 \times 102 = 1020\text{g}$$

The equation shows that one mole of aluminium oxide produces two moles of aluminium.

$$\text{amount of aluminium} = \frac{\text{mass}}{\text{atomic mass}}$$

Relative atomic masses (A_r): Al = 27 and O = 16.

The equation shows that one mole of aluminium oxide is needed to produce two moles of aluminium, so divide by two.

- The numbers needed to balance an equation can be calculated from the masses of the reactants and the products using moles.

mass of aluminium oxide needed = amount (mol) × formula mass

In a chemical reaction, 72g of magnesium was reacted with exactly 48g of oxygen molecules to produce 120g of magnesium oxide.

Use the number of moles of reactants and products to write a balanced equation for the reaction.

$$\text{amount of Mg} = \frac{72}{24} = 3\text{mol}$$

$$\text{amount of O}_2 = \frac{48}{32} = 1.5\text{mol}$$

$$\text{amount of MgO} = \frac{120}{40} = 3\text{mol}$$

$$3Mg + 1.5O_2 \rightarrow 3MgO$$

$$2Mg + O_2 \rightarrow 2MgO$$

Use the masses of the reactants to calculate the number of moles present.

Divide the number of moles of each substance by the smallest number (1.5) to give the simplest whole number ratio.

This shows that 2 moles of magnesium react with 1 mole of oxygen molecules to produce 2 moles of magnesium oxide.

Limiting Reactants

- Sometimes when two chemicals react together, one chemical is completely used up during the reaction.
- When one chemical is used up, it stops the reaction going any further. It is called the limiting reactant.
- The other chemical, which is not used up, is said to be in excess.

Moles of a Gas

- At room temperature and pressure, one mole of any gas takes up a volume of 24dm³.
- At room temperature and pressure:

volume = amount (mol) × 24dm³

HT **Quick Test**

1. 69g of sodium reacts with chlorine to produce sodium chloride:
$$2Na + Cl_2 \rightarrow 2NaCl$$
   a) Calculate the number of moles of sodium present.
   b) Calculate the number of moles of chlorine (Cl_2) that would be required to react exactly with the sodium.
   c) Calculate the mass of chlorine that would be required to react exactly with the sodium.

 Key Words

mole (mol)
Avogadro constant
limiting reactant

Titration

You must be able to:

- HT Recall the units for calculating the concentration of solutions
- HT Be able to work out the amount of solute in a solution of known volume and concentration
- HT Describe how to carry out a titration using a strong acid and a strong alkali
- HT Work out the concentration of a solution using data from titrations.

Concentration

- The concentration of a solution is often measured using units of mol/dm³.

 LEARN HT concentration of a solution = $\dfrac{\text{amount of substance (mol)}}{\text{volume (dm}^3\text{)}}$

 Key Point

There are 1000cm³ in 1.00dm³, so 500cm³ has a volume of 0.500dm³.

- If 1.00 mole of solute is dissolved to form a solution that has a volume of 1.00dm³, the solution has a concentration of 1.00mol/dm³.

> 2.00dm³ of sodium hydroxide solution contains 0.50 moles of sodium hydroxide.
> Work out the concentration of the solution.
>
> concentration of a solution = $\dfrac{\text{amount of substance (mol)}}{\text{volume (dm}^3\text{)}}$
>
> $= \dfrac{0.50\text{mol}}{2.00\text{dm}^3} = 0.25\text{mol/dm}^3$ ◄—— Substitute the values into the formula.

- Occasionally concentrations are expressed in g/dm³.
- If 10.0g solute is dissolved to form a solution that has a volume of 1.00dm³, the solution has a concentration of 10.0g/dm³.

 Key Point

The concentration of a solution is found by dividing the amount of substance (in moles or grams) by the volume (in dm³).

Carrying Out a Titration

- Acids and alkalis react together to form a neutral solution.
- Titration is an accurate technique that can be used to find out how much of an acid is needed to neutralise an alkali.
- When neutralisation takes place, the hydrogen ions (H⁺) from the acid join with the hydroxide ions (OH⁻) from the alkali to form water (neutral pH).

$$H^+(aq) + OH^-(aq) \longrightarrow H_2O(l)$$

- You must use a suitable indicator in titrations.
- If you have a strong acid and strong alkali, you could use methyl orange or phenolphthalein.
- Hydrochloric acid, nitric acid and sulfuric acid are all strong acids.
- Aqueous sodium hydroxide and aqueous potassium hydroxide are strong alkalis.

 Key Point

Indicators are one colour in acids and another colour in alkalis. They are used to show the end point of the titration.

REQUIRED PRACTICAL

Determination of the reacting volumes of solutions of a strong acid and a strong alkali by titration.

Sample Method	Hazards and Risks
1. Wash and rinse a pipette with the alkali being used. 2. Use the pipette to measure out a known and accurate volume of the alkali. 3. Place the alkali in a clean, dry conical flask. 4. Add a suitable indicator, e.g. phenolphthalein. 5. Place the flask on a white tile so the colour can be seen clearly. 6. Place the acid in a burette that has been carefully washed and rinsed with the acid. 7. Take a reading of the volume of acid in the burette (initial reading). 8. Carefully add the acid to the alkali, swirling the flask to thoroughly mix. 9. Continue until the indicator just changes colour. This is called the end point. 10. Take a reading of the volume of acid in the burette (final reading). 11. Calculate the volume of acid added (i.e. subtract the initial reading from the final reading).	• Acids and alkalis can damage the skin or eyes, so eye protection must be worn and any spillages wiped up.

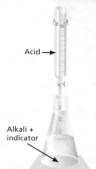

Acid →

Alkali + indicator

Titration can be used to find the concentration of an acid or alkali, providing the following are known:
- the relative volumes of acid and alkali used
- the concentration of the other acid or alkali.

Break down the calculation:

1 Write down a balanced equation for the reaction to determine the ratio of moles of acid to alkali involved.

2 Calculate the number of moles in the solution of known volume and concentration. You can work out the number of moles in the other solution from the balanced equation.

3 Calculate the concentration of the other solution.

> **HT Key Point**
>
> This method can be repeated to check results and can then be performed without an indicator in order to obtain the salt.

A titration is carried out and 0.04dm³ hydrochloric acid neutralises 0.08dm³ sodium hydroxide of concentration 1.00mol/dm³.

Calculate the concentration of the hydrochloric acid.

$$HCl + NaOH \rightarrow NaCl + H_2O$$

Write the balanced symbol equation for the reaction.

number of moles of NaOH = volume × concentration

$$= 0.08dm^3 \times 1.00mol/dm^3 = 0.08mol$$

$$\text{concentration of HCl} = \frac{\text{number of moles of HCl}}{\text{volume of HCl}}$$

$$= \frac{0.08mol}{0.04dm^3} = 2.00mol/dm^3$$

The balanced equation shows that the amount of hydrochloric acid is equal to the amount of sodium hydroxide, i.e. 0.08mol.

HT Quick Test

1. 1.50 moles of solute is dissolved in 1.00dm³ of solution. What is the concentration of the solution?
2. 2.00g of solute is dissolved in 2.00dm³ of solution. What is the concentration of the solution?
3. 0.20 moles of solute is dissolved in 500cm³ of solution. What is the concentration of the solution?

> **HT Key Words**
>
> concentration
> solute
> titration
> indicator

Percentage Yield and Atom Economy

You must be able to:

- Explain why a reaction may not produce the theoretical yield of the product
- Calculate the percentage yield for a reaction
- Calculate the atom economy of a reaction
- **HT** Explain why a particular reaction pathway may be chosen, using appropriate information.

Percentage Yield

- Atoms are never lost or gained in a chemical reaction.
- However, it is *not* always possible to obtain the calculated amount of product:
  - If the reaction is reversible, it might not go to completion.
  - Some product could be lost when it is separated from the reaction mixture.
  - Some of the reactants may react in different ways to the expected reaction.
- The amount of product obtained is called the yield.
- The percentage yield can be calculated using the formula:

$$\text{percentage yield} = \frac{\text{yield from reaction}}{\text{maximum theoretical yield}} \times 100$$

> ### Key Point
>
> Percentage yield is used to compare the actual yield obtained from a reaction with the maximum theoretical yield.
>
> A percentage yield of 100% would mean that no product had been lost.

Calculating Yield

Relative atomic masses (A_r):
Ca = 40, C = 12, O = 16

Calculate how much calcium oxide can be produced from 50.0kg of calcium carbonate.

$$CaCO_3 \rightarrow CaO + CO_2$$
$$[40 + 12 + (3 \times 16)] \rightarrow [40 + 16] + [12 + (2 \times 16)]$$
$$100 \rightarrow 56 + 44$$

100 : 56
100kg of $CaCO_3$ produces 56kg of CaO

So, 1kg of $CaCO_3$ produces $\frac{56}{100}$ = 0.56kg of CaO

And, 50kg of $CaCO_3$ produces 0.56 × 50 = 28kg of CaO

Write down the equation.

Work out the M_r of each substance.

Check that the total mass of reactants equals the total mass of products. If they are not the same, check your work.

The question only mentions calcium oxide and calcium carbonate, so you can now ignore the carbon dioxide. You just need the ratio of mass of reactant to mass of product.

Use the ratio to calculate how much calcium oxide can be produced.

50kg of calcium carbonate ($CaCO_3$) is expected to produce 28kg of calcium oxide (CaO).
A company heats 50kg of calcium carbonate in a kiln and obtains 22kg of calcium oxide. Calculate the percentage yield.

$$\text{percentage yield} = \frac{22}{28} \times 100 = 78.6\%$$

Atom Economy

- Atom economy is a measure of the amount of reactant that ends up in a useful product.
- Scientists try to choose reaction pathways that have a high atom economy.

- This is important for economic reasons and for sustainable development, as more products are made and less waste is produced.
- The percentage atom economy is calculated using the formula:

$$\text{atom economy} = \frac{\text{relative formula mass of the desired product}}{\text{sum of the relative formula mass of all the products/reactants}} \times 100$$

The Production of Ethanol

- Ethanol can be produced in two different ways: hydration and fermentation.
- During hydration, ethene is reacted with steam to form ethanol:

$$C_2H_4 + H_2O \longrightarrow C_2H_5OH$$

- The atom economy for the hydration method is 100%.
- The hydration of ethene is an addition reaction – all the reactant atoms end up in the desired product.
- Ethanol can also be produced by the fermentation of glucose:

$$C_6H_{12}O_6 \longrightarrow 2C_2H_5OH + 2CO_2 \longleftarrow$$

$$\text{atom economy} = \frac{92}{180} \times 100 = 51.1\%$$

- The atom economy for this reaction pathway is much lower – only about half of the atoms in the reactants end up in the desired product.

HT Choosing a Reaction Pathway

- Comparing the atom economy of two competing reaction pathways is important.
- However, it is just one of the factors that scientists have to consider when they choose which method to use.
- Important factors to consider when choosing a reaction pathway include:
  - the atom economy
  - cost of reactants
  - the percentage yield
  - the rate of reaction
  - the equilibrium position
  - the usefulness of by-products.

 Key Point

Sustainable development meets the needs of the current generation without compromising the ability of future generations to meet their own needs.

Key Point

Although the hydration of ethene has a high atom economy, ethene is produced from crude oil, which is non-renewable, and the process requires high temperatures, which can be expensive to maintain.

 Quick Test

1. Why might the actual yield of a reaction be less than the theoretical yield of the reaction?
2. A reaction has a theoretical yield of 13g but an actual yield of 8.5g. What is the percentage yield of this reaction?
3. Why are reactions that have a high atom economy good for the environment?
4. The equation for the formation of ammonia, NH_3, from its elements is shown below. What is the percentage atom economy of this reaction?
$$N_2 + 3H_2 \rightarrow 2NH_3$$

Key Words

percentage yield
atom economy
sustainable development
hydration
fermentation
addition reaction

Review Questions

States of Matter

1 State symbols are used to add extra information to equations.

    a) What does the state symbol (s) mean? [1]

    b) What does the state symbol (l) mean? [1]

Total Marks _____ / 2

Ionic Compounds

1 **Table 1** shows the charge of some metal ions and non-metal ions.

Table 1

Metal Ions	Non-Metal Ions
Lithium, Li^+	Oxide, O^{2-}
Strontium, Sr^{2+}	Chloride, Cl^-
Potassium, K^+	Bromide, Br^-
Magnesium, Mg^{2+}	Sulfide, S^{2-}

a) Define the term 'ion'. [2]

b) In terms of electron transfer, explain why lithium ions have a 1+ charge. [2]

c) In terms of electron transfer, explain why oxide ions have a 2– charge. [2]

    d) Use the table above to suggest the formula of:

        i) Strontium chloride. [1]

        ii) Potassium bromide. [1]

        iii) Magnesium sulfide. [1]

2 **Figure 1** shows the outer electrons in a sodium atom and in a chlorine atom.

Figure 1

    a)   **i)** In which group of the periodic table is sodium? [1]

        ii) In which group of the periodic table is chlorine? [1]

b) Draw a diagram to show the electronic structure of a sodium ion and a chloride ion.   [2]

Show the outer shell of electrons only.

c) The compound sodium chloride is a solid at room temperature.

i) What type of bonding is present in sodium chloride?   [1]

ii) Why is sodium chloride a solid at room temperature?   [2]

> **Total Marks** _____ / 16

Metals

1 Lithium reacts with chlorine to produce lithium chloride:

$2Li(s) + Cl_2(g) \rightarrow 2LiCl(s)$

a) What is the state of the:

i) Lithium?   **ii)** Chlorine?   [2]

b) What type of bonding is present in lithium?   [1]

c) Why is lithium a good electrical conductor?   [2]

d) What sort of bonding is present in chlorine molecules?   [1]

e) Why is chlorine a gas at room temperature?   [1]

f) The reaction produces lithium chloride.

What type of bonding is present in lithium chloride?   [1]

g) Lithium chloride does not conduct electricity when it is solid, but it does conduct electricity when it is molten. Explain why.   [2]

2 **a)** Name the type of bonding that occurs in copper.   [1]

b) Copper is used to make electrical wires because it is a very good electrical conductor.

Why is copper a good electrical conductor?   [2]

> **Total Marks** _____ / 13

Covalent Compounds

1 **Figure 1** shows the structure of graphite.

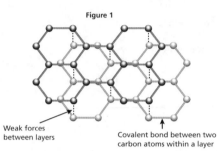

Figure 1

Weak forces between layers

Covalent bond between two carbon atoms within a layer

a) Graphite is a form of the element carbon.

Name **one** other form of carbon that is solid at room temperature. [1]

b) Within each layer of graphite, each carbon atom is bonded to other carbon atoms by strong bonds.

How many carbon atoms is each carbon atom joined to by strong bonds? [1]

c) Carbon in the form of graphite is the only non-metal that conducts electricity.

Explain why graphite can conduct electricity. [2]

d) Explain why graphite has a very high melting point. [2]

2 Ammonia molecules have the formula NH_3.

a) In which group of the periodic table is nitrogen? [1]

b) Ammonia has a low boiling point and is a gas at room temperature.

Explain why ammonia has a low boiling point. [2]

c) Explain why ammonia does not conduct electricity. [1]

3 **Figure 2** shows the structure of silicon dioxide.

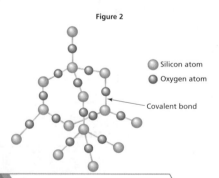

Figure 2

Silicon atom
Oxygen atom
Covalent bond

a) Silicon dioxide has the formula SiO_2.

   i) How many silicon atoms is each oxygen atom bonded to? [1]

   ii) How many oxygen atoms is each silicon atom bonded to? [1]

b) Silicon dioxide has a giant covalent structure.

   Why does silicon dioxide have a very high melting point? [2]

4 Methane, CH_4, and butane, C_4H_{10}, are both fuels with a simple molecular structure.

a) Name the type of bonding that occurs in methane and butane molecules. [1]

b) **Figure 4** shows the electronic structure of a carbon atom and a hydrogen atom.

Figure 4

Complete **Figure 5** to show the electron arrangement in a methane molecule.

Figure 5

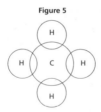

[1]

c) Which fuel – methane or butane – has the higher boiling point?
You must explain your answer. [3]

> **Total Marks** .... / 19

Special Materials

1 Graphene was discovered in 2004.

a) What element makes up graphene? [1]

b) Describe the structure of graphene. [2]

> **Total Marks** .... / 3

Conservation of Mass

1 Sulfur dioxide is produced when sulfur is burned.
Relative atomic masses (A_r): S = 32, O = 16

    a) Calculate the relative molecular mass of sulfur dioxide, SO_2.   **[2]**

    b) ᴴᵀ Calculate the mass of 1.00 mole of sulfur dioxide, SO_2.   **[1]**

    c) ᴴᵀ Calculate the mass of 0.5 moles of sulfur dioxide, SO_2.   **[1]**

2 ᴴᵀ Magnesium is more reactive than copper.
Magnesium displaces copper from a solution of copper sulfate.
This reaction can be summed up by the balanced symbol equation below:

$$Mg + CuSO_4 \rightarrow MgSO_4 + Cu$$

This equation can be split into two half equations.

Complete the two half equations.

    a) $Mg \rightarrow Mg^{2+} +$ ....   **[1]**

    b) $Cu^{2+} +$ .... $\rightarrow$ ....   **[2]**

3 What is the relative formula mass of $Ca(NO_3)_2$?
Relative atomic masses (A_r): Ca = 40, N = 14, O = 16
Tick **one** box.

164   ☐

164g   ☐

150   ☐

150g   ☐   **[1]**

4 A student adds a piece of magnesium ribbon to a flask of dilute hydrochloric acid.

$$Mg(s) + 2HCl(aq) \rightarrow MgCl_2(aq) + H_2(g)$$

Why does the mass of the reaction flask go down?   **[2]**

Total Marks .... **/ 10**

HT Amount of Substance

1 What unit do chemists use to measure the amount of substance?
Tick **one** box.

Grams ☐ Moles ☐

Kilograms ☐ Tonnes ☐ [1]

2 The Avogadro constant has a value of 6.02×10^{23}.

a) How many atoms are present in 7g of lithium? [1]

b) How many atoms are present in 24g of carbon? [1]

3 Calculate the number of moles in each of these substances:

a) 19g of fluorine, F_2. [2]

b) 22g of carbon dioxide, CO_2. [2]

c) 17g of hydroxide, OH^- ions. [2]

4 Complete combustion of carbon produces carbon dioxide, CO_2.

$C + O_2 \rightarrow CO_2$

1.8g of carbon was completely burned in oxygen.
Relative atomic masses (A_r): C = 12, O = 16

a) How many moles of carbon were burned? [2]

b) Calculate the mass of carbon dioxide, CO_2, produced in this reaction. [2]

5 When a hydrogen balloon explodes, the hydrogen reacts with an excess of oxygen
to produce water vapour.

$2H_2 + O_2 \rightarrow 2H_2O$

1.8g of water vapour was produced in this reaction.

a) What does the term 'excess' mean? [1]

b) Calculate the amount, in moles, of water vapour produced in this reaction. [2]

c) Calculate the amount, in moles, of hydrogen that reacted in this reaction. [1]

d) Calculate the mass of hydrogen that would produce 1.8g of water vapour. [2]

6 At room temperature and pressure, 1 mole of any gas takes up a volume of $24dm^3$.

a) Calculate the volume that 0.6 moles of fluorine, F_2, occupies. [2]

b) Calculate the amount, in moles, of methane, CH_4, gas present in $6dm^3$ at room temperature and pressure. [2]

7 When magnesium is heated it reacts to produce magnesium oxide.

$$2Mg(s) + O_2(g) \rightarrow 2MgO(s)$$

a) What is meant by 'conservation of mass'? [1]

b) What does the state symbol (g) mean? [1]

c) 1.2g of magnesium was heated until it had all reacted.
2.0g of magnesium oxide was produced.

Why has the mass of the solid gone up? [2]

d) Calculate the mass of oxygen that reacted with magnesium in this reaction. [1]

8 Copper hydroxide is an ionic compound.
Relative atomic masses (A_r): Cu = 63.5, O = 16, H = 1

a) Calculate the relative formula mass of copper hydroxide, $Cu(OH)_2$. [2]

b) Calculate the mass of 1.00 mole of copper hydroxide, $Cu(OH)_2$. [1]

Total Marks _____ / 31

HT Titration

1 A student makes a solution of copper sulfate.
They place 0.100 mole of copper sulfate crystals in a volumetric flask.
They then add distilled water until the solution has a volume of $1.00dm^3$.

What is the concentration of this solution?
You must give the unit. [2]

2 Titration can be used to measure how much alkali is needed to neutralise an acid.

20.0cm³ of potassium hydroxide was placed in a flask.
The potassium hydroxide has a concentration of 0.2mol/dm³.
This required 18.0cm³ of nitric acid solution for complete neutralisation.
The equation for the reaction can be summed up by the equation:

$$HNO_3 + KOH \rightarrow KNO_3 + H_2O$$

a) How many moles of potassium hydroxide were used in this reaction?   [2]

b) How many moles of nitric acid were used in this reaction?   [1]

c) What was the concentration of the nitric acid?   [2]

Total Marks _____ / 7

Percentage Yield and Atom Economy

1 A chemist expected a reaction to produce 12.0g of product.
However, after carrying out the reaction only 9.5g of product was actually produced.

a) Why might the actual yield of a reaction be less than the theoretical yield of the product?
Tick **one** box.

The reaction is reversible and does not go to completion.   ☐

One reactant is in excess.   ☐

One reactant is limiting the reaction.   ☐

A reaction has an atom economy of less than 100%.   ☐   [1]

b) Calculate the percentage yield of this reaction.
Give your answer to the nearest whole number.   [2]

Total Marks _____ / 3

Conservation of Mass

1 Carbon dioxide is produced when carbon is burned in a good supply of oxygen.

Relative atomic masses (A_r): C = 12, O = 16

a) Calculate the relative molecular mass of carbon dioxide, CO_2. [2]

b) HT Calculate the mass of 1.00 mole of carbon dioxide, CO_2. [1]

c) HT Calculate the mass of 2.00 moles of carbon dioxide, CO_2. [1]

2 HT Zinc is more reactive than iron.
Zinc displaces iron from a solution of iron sulfate solution:

$$Zn + FeSO_4 \rightarrow ZnSO_4 + Fe$$

Complete the two half equations for this reaction:

[1]

a) ..... $\rightarrow Zn^{2+} + 2e^-$

[2]

b) $Fe^{2+} +$ ..... $\rightarrow$ .....

3 When calcium carbonate is heated fiercely, it decomposes to form calcium oxide and carbon dioxide.

$$CaCO_3(s) \rightarrow CaO(s) + CO_2(g)$$

a) Why is the total mass of the reactants before the reaction equal to the total mass of reactants after the reaction? [1]

b) What does the state symbol (s) mean? [1]

c) 10.0g of calcium carbonate was heated until it had all reacted.
5.6g of calcium oxide was produced.

Why has the mass of the solid gone down? [2]

d) Predict the mass of carbon dioxide produced in this reaction. [1]

4 Water vapour is produced when hydrogen is burned in a good supply of oxygen.
Relative atomic masses (A_r): H = 1, O = 16

a) Calculate the relative formula mass of water, H_2O. [2

b) HT Calculate the mass of 0.50 moles of water, H_2O. [2

5 Magnesium nitrate is an ionic compound.
Relative atomic masses (A_r): Mg = 24, N = 14, O = 16

a) Calculate the relative formula mass of magnesium nitrate, $Mg(NO_3)_2$. [2]

b) HT Calculate the mass of 1.00 mole of magnesium nitrate, $Mg(NO_3)_2$. [1]

6 A student places a piece of magnesium ribbon in a crucible.
They carefully heat the crucible and the magnesium.

$$2Mg(s) + O_2(g) \rightarrow 2MgO(s)$$

Why does the mass of the crucible go up? [2]

Total Marks _____ / 21

HT Amount of Substance

1 What is the Avogadro constant?
Tick **one** box.

The number of particles in 1g of a substance. ☐

The number of particles in 1 mole of a substance. ☐

The number of protons in 1 mole of carbon. ☐

The number of subatomic particles in 1 mole of carbon. ☐ [1]

2 The Avogadro constant has a value of 6.02×10^{23}.

a) How many atoms are present in 23g of sodium? [1]

b) How many atoms are present in 6g of carbon? [1]

3 Calculate the number of moles in each of these substances:

a) 39g of potassium. [1]

b) 32g of sulfur dioxide, SO_2. [2]

c) 18g of ammonium ions, NH_4^+. [2]

4 Many fuels contain small amounts of sulfur.
When sulfur is burned, sulfur dioxide, SO_2, is produced

$$S + O_2 \rightarrow SO_2$$

1.6g of sulfur was completely burned in oxygen to produce sulfur dioxide.
Relative atomic masses (A_r): S = 32, O = 16

a) How many moles of sulfur were burned? [2]

b) Calculate the mass of sulfur dioxide, SO_2, produced in this reaction. [2]

5 Hydrogen was reacted with an excess of chlorine to produce hydrogen chloride.

$$H_2 + Cl_2 \rightarrow 2HCl$$

0.73g of hydrogen chloride was produced in this reaction.

a) Calculate the amount, in moles, of hydrogen chloride produced in this reaction. [2]

b) Calculate the amount, in moles, of hydrogen that reacted in this reaction. [2]

c) Calculate the mass of hydrogen that would produce 0.73g of hydrogen chloride. [2]

6 At room temperature and pressure, 1 mole of any gas takes up a volume of $24dm^3$.

a) Calculate the volume of 0.2 moles of nitrogen, N_2. [2]

b) Calculate the amount, in moles, of oxygen, O_2, gas present in $18dm^3$ at room
temperature and pressure. [2]

Total Marks _____ / 22

HT Titration

1 A student makes a solution of sodium hydroxide.
They place 1.00 mole of sodium hydroxide pellets in a volumetric flask.
They then add distilled water until the solution has a volume of $500cm^3$.
What is the concentration of this solution?
You must include the units in your answer. [2]

2   Titration can be used to measure how much alkali is needed to neutralise an acid.

25.0cm³ of sodium hydroxide was placed in a flask.
The sodium hydroxide has a concentration of 0.1mol/dm³.
This required 22.5cm³ of hydrochloric acid solution for complete neutralisation.
The reaction can be summed up by the equation:

$$HCl + NaOH \rightarrow NaCl + H_2O$$

a) How many moles of sodium hydroxide were used in this reaction?   [2]

b) How many moles of hydrochloric acid were used in this reaction?   [1]

c) What is the concentration of the hydrochloric acid?   [2]

Total Marks _____ / 7

Percentage Yield and Atom Economy

1   The theoretical yield of a reaction is 15.0g of product.
A chemist carries out the reaction and produces only 9.0g of product.

Calculate the percentage yield of this reaction.   [2]

2   Copper is a very useful metal.
It can be extracted from a solution of copper sulfate using scrap iron.
Relative formula mass (A_r): Fe = 56, Cu = 63.5, S = 32, O = 16

$$Fe + CuSO_4 \rightarrow Cu + FeSO_4$$

Reactions with a high atom economy contribute towards sustainable development.

a) Name the products of the reaction.   [2]

b) Calculate the relative formula mass of iron sulfate, $FeSO_4$.   [2]

c) Calculate the percentage atom economy of this reaction.
Give your answer to the nearest whole number.   [2]

Total Marks _____ / 8

Answers

Page 5 Quick Test
1. Liquid
2. Aqueous / dissolved in water
3. Quickly and randomly in all directions
4. To melt, the strong bonds between the ions must be broken. This requires lots of energy, so it only happens at high temperatures.
5. The particle model does not take into account: the forces between the particles; the volume of the particles; or the space between particles.

Page 7 Quick Test
1. Atoms that have gained or lost electrons and now have an overall charge
2. They lose electrons
3. KCl
4. The ions in molten ionic compounds can move about, carrying their charge

Page 9 Quick Test
1. An attraction between the positive metal ions and the delocalised electrons
2. It is an unreactive metal, so it does not react with water, and it can be easily shaped
3. A mixture that contains a metal and at least one other element
4. They are usually stronger and harder than pure metals
5. Hard; resistant to corrosion

Page 11 Quick Test
1. A shared pair of electrons between atoms
2. It is a simple molecule – although there is a strong covalent bond within the molecule, there are only weak intermolecular forces between molecules
3. The larger the molecule, the stronger the intermolecular forces between molecules
4. Each carbon atom forms four strong covalent bonds with other carbon atoms
5. The delocalised electrons can move and carry their charge

Page 13 Quick Test
1. It is a single layer of graphite, just one atom thick
2. Buckminsterfullerene
3. 1–100nm / a few hundred atoms in size
4. They could potentially damage human cells or the environment

Page 14 States of Matter
1. a) Gas [1]
   b) Aqueous / dissolved in water [1]
2. It does not take into account the: forces between the particles [1]; that particles, although small, do have some volume [1]; the space between particles [1]

3. a) Solid [1]
   b) Aqueous / dissolved in water [1]
   c) Gas [1]

Page 14 Ionic Compounds
1. a) It contains lots of strong ionic bonds [1]; so lots of energy is needed to overcome the bonds [1]
   b) No, the ions cannot move in a solid [1]
   c) Yes, the ions can move in a molten state [1]
   d) Yes, the ions can move in an aqueous solution [1]
2. a) An atom that has gained or lost electrons [1]
   b) It has gained [1]; 1 electron [1]
   c) It has lost [1]; 2 electrons [1]
   d) i) KCl [1]
      ii) MgS [1]
      iii) CaO [1]

   Remember that compounds have no overall charge.

   e) It has lots of strong ionic bonds [1]; so lots of energy is required to overcome these bonds [1]

Page 15 Metals
1. a) Au [1]

   Use your periodic table if you need to.

   b) Metallic [1]
   c) Atoms form layers [1]; that can slip over each other [1]
   d) A mixture that contains at least one metal [1]
   e) It has delocalised / free electrons [1]; that can move [1]

Page 16 Covalent Compounds
1. a) Carbon [1]
   b) It has lots of strong covalent bonds [1]
   c) It contains no charged particles [1]
2. a) It contains no charged particles [1]
   b) There are only weak forces of attraction between methane molecules [1]; that are easily overcome [1]
3. a) i) Group 2 [1]
      ii) Group 6 [1]
      iii) Correctly drawn outer electrons of a magnesium ion [1]; and sulfide ion [1]

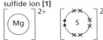

   b) Giant ionic [1]
   c) The ions [1]; cannot move in a solid [1]

4. a) A shared pair of electrons [1]
   b) Correctly drawn diagram [1]

   c) They contain no charged particles [1]

Page 17 Special Materials
1. a) 1 to 100nm [1]
   b) They could get into and damage human cells / damage the environment [1]

Page 19 Quick Test
1. The total mass of the products of a chemical reaction is always equal to the total mass of the reactants.
2. Because no atoms are lost or made, the products of a chemical reaction are made from exactly the same atoms as the reactants.
3. $(1 \times 2) + 16 = 18$
4. $40 + 12 + (16 \times 3) = 100$
5. Because the iron combines with oxygen in the air and the oxygen has mass

Page 21 Quick Test
1. a) $\frac{69}{23} = 3$ moles
   b) $\frac{3}{2} = 1.5$ moles
   c) $1.5 \times (35.5 \times 2) = 106.5g$

Page 23 Quick Test
1. $\frac{1.50}{1.00} = 1.50 mol/dm^3$
2. $\frac{2.00}{2.00} = 1.00 g/dm^3$
3. $\frac{0.20}{0.50} = 0.40 mol/dm^3$

Page 25 Quick Test
1. If the reaction is reversible and it does not go to completion; some product is lost when it is separated from the reaction mixture; some of the reactants react in different ways to the expected reaction
2. percentage yield $= \frac{8.5}{13} \times 100 = 65.4\%$
3. They produce less waste material that could end up damaging the environment
4. 100% (there is only one product)

Page 26 States of Matter

1. a) Solid **[1]**
   b) Liquid **[1]**

Page 26 Ionic Compounds

1. a) An atom that has gained **[1]**; or lost electrons **[1]**
   b) It has lost **[1]**; one electron **[1]**
   c) It has gained **[1]**; two electrons **[1]**
   d) i) $SrCl_2$ **[1]**
      ii) KBr **[1]**
      iii) MgS **[1]**

2. a) i) Group 1 / alkali metals **[1]**
      ii) Group 7 / halogens **[1]**

   b) Correct dot and cross diagrams **[1]**; correct charges **[1]**

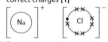

   c) i) Ionic **[1]**
      ii) Lots of strong bonds **[1]**; lots of energy is needed to overcome them **[1]**

Page 27 Metals

1. a) i) Solid **[1]**
      ii) Gas **[1]**
   b) Metallic **[1]**
   c) It has delocalised / free electrons **[1]**; that can move **[1]**
   d) Covalent **[1]**
   e) Only weak forces of attraction between the chlorine molecules **[1]**
   f) Ionic **[1]**
   g) When solid the ions cannot move **[1]**; when molten the ions can move **[1]**

2. a) Metallic **[1]**
   b) Delocalised / free electrons **[1]**; which can move **[1]**

Page 28 Covalent Compounds

1. a) Diamond / graphene / nanotubes **[1]**
   b) 3 **[1]**
   c) It has delocalised / free electrons **[1]**; that can move **[1]**
   d) It has lots of strong covalent bonds **[1]**; and lots of energy is required to overcome these forces of attraction **[1]**

2. a) Group 5 **[1]**
   b) There are only weak forces of attraction between particles **[1]**; which are easily overcome, so little energy is required **[1]**
   c) It does not contain any charged particles **[1]**

3. a) i) 2 **[1]**
      ii) 4 **[1]**
   b) It contains lots of strong covalent bonds **[1]**; so lots of energy is needed to break the bonds **[1]**

4. a) Covalent **[1]**
   b) Correctly drawn diagram **[1]**

   c) Butane **[1]**; it is a larger molecule **[1]**; so there are stronger forces of attraction between butane molecules **[1]**

Page 29 Special Materials

1. a) Carbon **[1]**
   b) A single layer / one atom thick of graphite **[1]**; carbons are in a hexagonal structure / honeycomb structure **[1]**

Page 30 Conservation of Mass

1. a) $32 + (2 \times 16)$ **[1]**; $= 64$ **[1]**
   b) 64g **[1]**
   c) 32g **[1]**
2. a) $2e^-$ **[1]**
   b) $2e^-$ **[1]**; Cu **[1]**
3. 164 **[1]**
4. Hydrogen / a gas is made **[1]**; and it escapes from the flask **[1]**

Page 31 Amount of Substance

1. Moles **[1]**
2. a) 6.02×10^{23} **[1]**
   b) 1.204×10^{24} **[1]**

> Remember, one mole of any substance contains 6×10^{23} atoms.

3. a) $\frac{19}{38}$ **[1]**; 0.5mol **[1]**
   b) $\frac{22}{44}$ **[1]**; 0.5mol **[1]**
   c) $\frac{17}{17}$ **[1]**; 1.0mol **[1]**
4. a) $\frac{1.8}{12}$ **[1]**; $= 0.15$mol **[1]**
   b) 44 **[1]**; $0.15 \times 44 = 6.6$g **[1]**
5. a) There is more than enough / some is left over **[1]**
   b) $\frac{1.8}{18}$ **[1]**; $= 0.1$mol **[1]**
   c) 0.1mol (same as number of moles of water vapour produced) **[1]**
   d) 0.1×2 **[1]**; $= 0.2$g **[1]**
6. a) 0.6×24 **[1]**; $= 14.4$dm^3 **[1]**
   b) $\frac{6}{24}$ **[1]**; $= 0.25$mol **[1]**

7. a) The total mass of the reactants is equal to the total mass of the products / no mass is gained or lost **[1]**
   b) Gas **[1]**
   c) It has reacted with oxygen **[1]**; oxygen has mass **[1]**
   d) $2.0 - 1.2 = 0.8$g **[1]**
8. a) $63.5 + ((16 + 1) \times 2)$ **[1]**; $= 97.5$ **[1]**
   b) 97.5g **[1]**

> One mole of a substance is the formula mass in grams.

Page 32 Titration

1. 0.1mol/dm^3 **[2]** (1 mark for correct value; 1 mark for correct unit)
2. a) $\frac{20}{1000} \times 0.2$ **[1]**; $0.02 \times 0.2 = 0.004$mol **[1]**
   b) 0.004mol **[1]**
   c) $\frac{0.004 \times 1000}{18}$ **[1]**; $= 0.22$mol/dm^3 **[1]**

Page 33 Percentage Yield and Atom Economy

1. a) The reaction is reversible and does not go to completion. **[1]**
   b) $\frac{9.5}{12}$ **[1]**; $= 79\%$ **[1]**

Page 34 Conservation of Mass

1. a) $12 + (2 \times 16)$ **[1]**; $= 44$ **[1]**
   b) 44g **[1]**
   c) 88g **[1]**
2. a) Zn **[1]**
   b) $2e^-$ **[1]**; Fe **[1]**
3. a) Mass is conserved / no atoms are gained or lost **[1]**
   b) Solid **[1]**
   c) Carbon dioxide / a gas is made **[1]**; and escapes **[1]**
   d) $10.0 - 5.6 = 4.4$g **[1]**

> Remember, total mass before = total mass after.

4. a) $(2 \times 1) + 16$ **[1]**; $= 18$ **[1]**
   b) 0.5×18 **[1]**; $= 9$g **[1]**
5. a) $24 + (14 + 48) \times 2$ **[1]**; $= 148$ **[1]**
   b) 148g **[1]**
6. Oxygen is added **[1]**; and oxygen has mass **[1]**

Page 35 Amount of Substance

1. The number of particles in 1 mole of a substance. **[1]**
2. a) 23g = 1 mole = 6.02×10^{23} atoms **[1]**

> First calculate the number of moles.

   b) 6g = 0.5 moles, so $6.02 \times 10^{23} \times 0.5 = 3.01 \times 10^{23}$ atoms **[1]**

Answers

3. a) $\frac{39}{39}$ = 1.00mol   [1]

   b) $\frac{32}{64}$ [1]; 0.5mol [1]

   c) $\frac{18}{18}$ [1]; 1.0mol [1]

4. a) $\frac{1.6}{32}$ [1]; = 0.05mol [1]

   b) 64g [1]; 0.05 × 64 = 3.2g [1]

5. a) $\frac{0.73}{36.5}$ [1]; = 0.02mol [1]

   b) $\frac{0.02}{2}$ [1]; = 0.01mol [1]

   c) 0.01 × 2 [1]; = 0.02g [1]

6. a) 0.2 × 24 [1]; 4.8dm³ [1]

   b) $\frac{18}{24}$ [1]; = 0.75mol [1]

Page 36 Titration

1. $\frac{1}{0.5}$ [1]; = 2.00mol/dm³ [1]

2. a) $\frac{25}{1000}$ × 0.1 [1]; = 0.0025mol [1]

   b) 0.0025mol   [1]

   > Look at the overall equation.

   c) $\frac{0.0025 \times 1000}{22.5}$ [1]; = 0.11mol/dm³ [1]

Page 37 Percentage Yield and Atom Economy

1. $\frac{9}{15}$ [1]; = 60% [1]

2. a) Copper [1]; iron sulfate [1]

   b) 56 + 32 + (16 × 4) [1]; = 152 [1]

   c) $\frac{63.5}{63.5 + 152}$ [1]; = 29% [1]

Notes

Notes

Notes

Notes